Electronic Chart Symbols

An Annotated ECDIS Chart No. 1

Edited and annotated

by

David Burch

STARPATH

ISBN 978-0-914025-78-8

Published by

Starpath Publications

3050 NW 63rd Street, Seattle, WA 98107

www.starpathpublications.com

10 9   8   7   6   5   4   3   2   1

The content of this booklet was adopted from *NOAA Chart No. 1* and adapted to meet the *IHO Pub S-52* standards on ENC symbol presentation. Notable portions of the source material have been updated. Annotations on standard definitions appear in *[square brackets, using blue italic font]*.

Every effort has been made to assure that the symbols presented here correspond to those intended by national and international standards. But the official prescriptions for the symbol designs and rules for their presentation are very complex in some cases, so we cannot guarantee that there are no errors in the selection presented here. The author and publisher cannot assume liability for any damage or loss that might be related to the use of this booklet.

Contents

Preface 4

Electronic Chart Symbols.. 6

Help make NOAA ENC even better........................... 6

A. Mariners' Navigational Symbols.............................7

B. Positions, Distances, Directions, Compass....................... 15

C. Natural Features.. 17

D. Cultural Features 19

E. Landmarks... 21

F. Ports.. 24

H. Tides, Currents 29

I. Depths 30

J. Nature of the Seabed 35

K. Rocks, Wrecks, Obstructions, Aquaculture....................... 37

L. Offshore Installations... 40

M. Tracks, Routes 42

N. Areas, Limits 47

P. Lights 50

"Paper Chart" vs. Simplified Symbols 54

Q. Buoys, Beacons 56

R. Fog Signals 65

S. Radar, Radio, Satellite Navigation Systems....................... 66

T. Services.. 68

Appendix: ENC Objects and Attributes 69

Other books by the author on ENC 76

Preface

Nautical charting in the U.S. is in the process of a major transition—one that is taking place in all maritime nations, but the U.S. is notably in the lead. All traditional NOAA paper charts will be discontinued by the end of 2024, replaced with electronic navigational charts (ENC) that are updated weekly. Even the ENC are being significantly improved with new gridding and scale standards in a process called *rescheming*. Based on all public information available, at the end of 2024, ENC will be the only official NOAA nautical charts.

NOAA Custom Charts (NCC)

For unofficial backup paper charts, mariners can use the new *NOAA Custom Charts (NCC)* that mariners create online using the NOAA NCC app. Any region, scale, or paper size can be selected to create a high-res PDF that the user then downloads and prints on their own—or they use one of the existing print on demand outlets that will transition to this service. See www.starpath.com/NCC.

NCC are based on the corresponding ENC, but NOAA has chosen to present these using the historic paper chart symbols, which are based on the *International Hydrographic Office (IHO) Pub. S-4, Standards for Paper Chart Symbols* (www.iho.int) plus their own NOAA versions that are presented in *NOAA Chart No. 1*.

IHO Standards
S-57 (ENC Content), and S-52 (ENC Display)

The IHO also provides the S-57 standard for what is included in an ENC and they provide the S-52 standard for how the ENC data should be presented on the mariner's electronic chart screen. By definition, an ENC is an S-57 compliant product. All ENC worldwide follow the same S-57 standard. Third-party electronic charts are not ENC. Their chart symbols vary with the companies making them. They do not meet carriage requirements and all include the warning that they should only be used in conjunction with official nautical charts, meaning ENC.

The S-52 display standard provides two options for chart symbols. One is called "paper chart" symbols and the other is called "simplified" symbols. The distinctions between these two options are shown throughout this booklet. But the S-52 designation of "paper chart" style does not at all match the actual paper chart symbols in use on paper charts around the world as specified in IHO Pub. S-4, which are usually referred to as the INT symbol set. Thus we have in effect at the moment three distinct sets of nautical chart symbols, which means learning chart reading is not as easy as it used to be! The main differences are the important symbols for aids to navigation.

With that in mind, we have included for each ENC symbol the corresponding symbol designation in the traditional INT system presented in Pub. S-4 and in the various *Chart No.1* publications around the world, and now used in the NCC.

ECDIS vs. ECS

How official ENC symbols are presented depends on how they are viewed. Large commercial and governmental vessels use an electronic navigation system called ECDIS (electronic chart and display information system). An ECDIS display is required to use the official S-52 standards shown in this booklet. Each vessel then decides if they want to use the "paper chart" or "simplified" S-52 symbols option.

Other (non-ECDIS) vessels view ENC on what is called an *electronic chart system (ECS)*. An ECS is any charting system that is not a *type-approved* ECDIS. Most ECS strive to match the S-52 display standards as a base line, but do not follow all requirements or conventions. Light symbol displays is one area where ECS might differ the most from ECDIS; rules on the implementation of the important isolated danger symbol may also vary, among others.

ENC Objects and Attributes

The official ENC symbols and their meanings are just the starting point to reading an ENC. Unlike paper charts, there is much more information included in an ENC than we can read on any screen display. "Chart reading" with ENC is an interactive process. We must *cursor pick* each symbol we care about to learn its detailed meaning. Put your cursor over the symbol and click or tap to open a window that lists the properties of that symbol and other underlying features at that location on the screen.

Everything on an ENC is called an *object* and every object has a list of *attributes* that further define it. All objects and attributes have unique six-letter abbreviations called *acronyms*. Thus when cursor picking a buoy symbol, we might learn that this is a lateral buoy object (BOYLAT) with attributes: Buoy shape (BOYSHP), Category of lateral mark (CATLAM), Color (COLOUR), Color pattern (COLPAT), and more. The *pick report* would include all of this information plus underlying objects such as: Depth area (DEPARE), Sea area (SEAARE), Magnetic variation (MAGVAR), and so on.

An ENC includes not just the traditional chart information but also much of the associated *Light List* and often some of the associated *Coast Pilot*. A list of all ENC objects and attributes is in the Appendix. From that we can learn what all might be known about a specific object, although all possible attributes are not likely to be encoded. As time goes by, more attributes will be reported to NOAA and then encoded. ENC are updated every Thursday morning, EST.

To learn more of the relationship between objects and attributes along with the definitions of each, see the excellent online object catalog from Caris:

www.caris.com/s-57

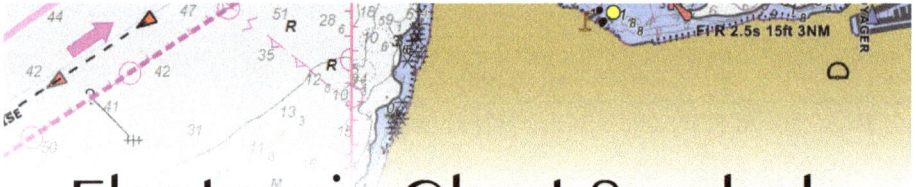

Electronic Chart Symbols

The IHO S-52 symbols presented here are intended to be used when displaying ENC from any maritime nation. These are the official international electronic chart symbols. ECDIS systems always use these symbols; ECS displaying ENC usually use these symbols, but may show occasional variations.

Third-party (commercial) charts are not official nautical charts, meaning they are not ENC. They have their own symbol styles depending on the company producing them. They are similar to these official symbols in most cases, but not identical.

In the tables that follow, columns have the format shown below, where INT/NCC refer to the IHO S-4 standard paper chart counterparts, which are also used in NOAA Custom Charts (NCC).

Symbol	Short description	INT/NCC
☉	Land as a point at small scale	K 10
◉ 8 m	Land as an area, with an elevation or control point	K 10
✳	Rock which covers and uncovers or is awash at low water	K 11, K 12

Help make NOAA ENC even better...

NOAA ENC are certainly among the very best in the world, but all mariners can help make them even more valuable for navigation by reporting discrepancies and submitting more details (attributes) of charted objects. The ENC structure makes it very easy to add new information that will then automatically show in chart displays once the charts are updated onboard. NOAA updates the ENC every Thursday morning. Use this link to make reports:

www.nauticalcharts.noaa.gov/customer-service/assist/

A. Mariners' Navigational Symbols

[Section A symbols do not have a paper chart counterpart. These displays are determined by the ECS or ECDIS. They are similar for all ECDIS, but differ notably among ECS.]

AIS *[Automatic Identification System]*	
△ △ ▲	Sleeping AIS target
△ △ ▲	Active AIS target
△ △ ▲	Dangerous AIS target
✕	Lost AIS target
⌐	AIS target turning to starboard
¬	AIS target turning to port
⬦⊕	AIS based aid to navigation
⬮	AIS target, true scale outline
⊗	AIS SART (Search and Rescue Transmitter) symbol
⊙	AIS base station

Examples of AIS Course Over Ground (COG), and Speed Over Ground (SOG) vector and targets	

Route Information *[ECDIS]*	
▬	Time mark on past track
▬	Time mark on secondary past track
⬭	Surrounding ellipse for arrival date and time at planned position
▬	Cross line for planned position
▭	Box for speed to make good, planned route *[red]*
▭	Box for speed to make good, alternate route *[orange]*
○	Waypoint on planned route *[red]*
○	Waypoint on alternate planned route *[orange]*
◎	Next waypoint on planned route
• • • • • • • • • • • • • • • •	Planned route for own ship

Example of route and waypoints	Example of past tracks

Manual Update Information	
	This object or line has been manually deleted or modified
	This object has been manually updated
	This line has been manually updated

Examples of manual updates

9

Chart Display Information	
┼	Ordinary cursor
	Cursor with open center
⬆N	North arrow
	Reference point, "ghost cursor" (user interface)
	One mile scale bar for display scales larger than 1:80,000 *[mile = nautical mile]* *[Many ECS use alternative styles.]*
	10 mile latitude scale for display scales smaller than 1:80,000 *[mile = nautical mile]* *[Many ECS use alternative styles.]*
	Chart scale boundary, the double line indicates the larger scale
	Overscale pattern *[Many ECS do not use this symbol.]*

Chart Tools	
	Arrowhead for mariners clearing line *[Danger Bearing]*
	Point of origin for an offset Electronic Bearing Line (EBL) or Variable Range Marker (VRM)
	Range mark for an Electronic Range and Bearing Line (ERBL)

Example of EBL and VRM offset, and own ship ERBL	Example of Clearing Line *[Danger Bearing]*

	Electronic Range and Bearing Line
	Own ship position fix
Radar Information	
	Automatic Radar Plotting Aid (ARPA) target
	One minute mark on an ARPA vector
	Six minute mark on an ARPA vector

⯍	Arrowhead for ARPA (or AIS) vector course and speed over ground
⌃	Arrowhead for ARPA (or AIS) vector course and speed through the water

Example of ARPA water vector
⊙⊢+ ⊢⊢⊢† ➔

Annotations	
[i]	Mariners' information note
(!)	Mariners' caution note
⊠	Mariners' event mark
[i]	Manufacturer's information note
(!)	Manufacturer's caution note
▢ ⊞	Transparent danger highlight for mariners' use
↑↑↑ ¦ ¦	Predicted tidal stream or current direction
⇑⇑⇑	Actual tidal stream or current direction

☐	P 3.2 ↑	Box for current strength

Own Ship Information *[ECDIS]*

—	One minute mark for own ship vector
—	Six minute mark for own ship vector
◎	Own ship symbol, constant size
⬭	Own ship drawn to scale with conning position marked
⟰	Arrowhead for own ship vector course and speed over ground
⌃	Arrowhead for own ship vector course and speed through the water

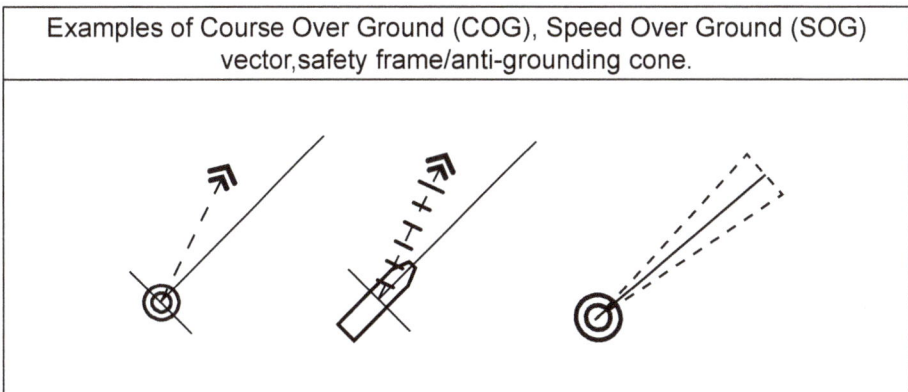

Examples of Course Over Ground (COG), Speed Over Ground (SOG) vector, safety frame/anti-grounding cone.

13

Zone of Confidence (ZOC) Categories

ZOC	SYMBOL	SOUNDING POSITION ACCURACY	DEPTH(d) ACCURACY	SEAFLOOR COVERAGE
A1		± 5 m +5% d ± 16.4 ft +5% d	0.50 m +1% d 1.6 ft +1% d	All significant seafloor features detected.
A2		± 20 m ± 65.6 ft	1.00 m +2% d 3.3 ft +2% d	All significant seafloor features detected.
B		± 50 m ± 164.0 ft	1.00 m +2% d 3.3 ft +2% d	Uncharted features hazardous to surface navigation are not expected but may exist.
C		± 500 m ± 1640.4 ft	2.00 m +2% d 6.6 ft +2% d	Depth anomalies may be expected.
D		Worse than ZOC C	Worse than ZOC C	Large depth anomalies may be expected.
U		Unassessed - The quality of the bathymetric data has yet to be assessed.		

[ZOC data are included on all NCC PDFs as well as in the ENC.]

B. Positions, Distances, Directions, Compass

Geographical Positions		INT/NCC
PA	Position approximate	B 7
?⟍	Point feature or area of low accuracy	B 7, 8
(21)	Sounding of low accuracy	B 7, 8
Control Points		
⊙	Position of an elevation or control point	B 20-24
km 7	Canal and distance point with no mark *[Unmarked distance point along a canal]*	B 25.1
○km 7	Canal and distance point *[Visible distance mark along a canal]*	B 25.2

Note: ENC use a magenta "km" symbol to represent distance marks. However, the distances shown along waterways on NOAA-produced ENC are displayed in statute miles.
[Rivers, Great Lakes, Intracoastal]

Symbolized Positions (Examples)		
ENC follow the paper chart convention for the position of symbols, except for simplified symbols for buoys and beacons (see Q 1).		B 30, 31
◉	Position of a point feature *[Brown when non-conspicuous]*	B 32

ENC indicate approximate position only for wrecks, obstructions, islets and shoreline features.		B 33
Magnetic Compass		
Varn	Magnetic Variation	B 60
9.54	Cursor pick site for magnetic variation at a point *[Point symbol includes the variation value; area symbols do not.]*	B 68.1, 70
	Cursor pick site for magnetic variation over an area	B 68.1
Varn - 3	Cursor pick site for magnetic variation along a line *[Example shown is 3° West. West is negative; East is positive.]*	B 71
	Cursor pick site for magnetic anomaly along a line or over an area	B 82.1, 82.2

C. Natural Features

Coastline		INT/NCC
	Coastline *[Nature of coastline (cliffs, etc.) is obtained by cursor pick.]*	C 1
	Coastline or shoreline construction of low accuracy in position *[Does not show if accuracy is not encoded]*	C 2
	Sloping ground crest line distant from coastline, radar or visually conspicuous	C 3
	Cliff as an area *[There are more cliff symbols on paper charts than on ENC.]*	C 3
	Conspicuous hill or mountain top *[Brown when non-conspicuous]*	C 4, C 8
Relief		
O 109 m	Elevation contour with spot height, contour value is obtained by cursor pick *[Many ENC do not show all elevation contours depicted on the corresponding paper chart.]*	C 10, 12-13
O 119 m	Position of an elevation or control point *[Spot elevations and contours on NOAA ENC are relative to MHW, not MSL as on paper charts.]*	C 11

Water Features, Lava

	River	C 20, 21
	Rapids Waterfall Waterfall, visually conspicuous	C 22
	Lake	C 23
	Continuous pattern for an ice area (glacier, etc.)	C 25

Vegetation

	Line of trees	C 30, 31.2, 31.3
	Wooded area	C 30, 31.5-8
	Tree *[Height of a tree is sometimes available by cursor pick.]*	C 31.1, 31.2
	Mangrove with coastline or shoreline construction of low accuracy in position	C 32
	Marsh with coastline or shoreline construction of low accuracy in position	C 33

D. Cultural Features

Settlements, Buildings		INT/NCC
	Built-up area	D 1
Name	Built-up area as a point	D 3, D 4
	Conspicuous single building *[Brown border when non-conspicuous]*	D 5
	Conspicuous single building in built-up area	D 6
Street names and status of ruins can be obtained by cursor pick		D 7, 8

Roads, Railways, Airfields		
	Road, track or path as a line	D 10-12
	Road as an area	D 10-12
	Railway, with station	D 13
	Cutting	D 14
	Embankment	D 15
	Embankment, visually or radar conspicuous	D 15

— — — — —	Tunnel	D 16
━ ━ ━ ━	Tunnel with depth below the seabed encoded	D 16
(airplane symbol)	Airport as a point	D 17
(crossed runways)	Runway as a line	D 17
(airport area with runway)	Airport area, with runway area and visually conspicuous runway area	D 17
clr 20.0 clr cl 20.0 clr op 20.0 sf clr 20.0	Vertical clearance Closed clearance Open clearance Safe clearance	D 20
clr 20.0 clr 20.0	Bridge	D 22, 23.5, 24
clr cl 8.2 clr op 20.0 clr cl 8.2 clr op 20.0	Opening bridge	D 23.1-4, 23.6
clr 20.0	Aerial or overhead cableway	D 25, 27
clr 20.0	Aerial or overhead cableway, radar conspicuous	D 25, 27
sf clr 20.0	Transmission line	D 26
sf clr 20.0	Transmission line, radar conspicuous	D 26

clr 20.0	Overhead pipeline	D 28
clr 20.0	Overhead pipeline, radar conspicuous	D 28
○— ○— ○—	Oil, gas pipeline, submerged or on land	D 29

E. Landmarks

[Height above ground level and/or above height datum is obtained by cursor pick. NOAA ENC include only one height datum; other nations use more.]

General		INT/NCC
⊙	Non-conspicuous point feature	E 1
▪	Non-conspicuous building	E 1
⬯	Non-conspicuous water tower	E 1
⊙	Conspicuous point feature	E 2, 12
■	Conspicuous building	E 2
⬯	Conspicuous water tower	E 2
1 ⬯	The information symbol is displayed if a supplemental image is available, which may be accessed by cursor pick *[NOAA ENC do not include images, but in principle they could be added by the user.]*	E 3.1

[NOAA ENC do not usually distinguish between conspicuous and non-conspicuous objects, but rare examples do exist.]

21

Landmarks		
	Church as a point, church tower, spire, dome, or chapel	E 10.1, 10.2-4, 11
	Church as an area	E 10.1
	Religious building, non-Christian	E 13-16
	Mosque or minaret	E 17, 18
	Landmark area	E 19
	Tower, radar tower	E 20
	Water tower	E 21
	Chimney	E 22
	Flare stack	E 23
	Monument	E 24
	Windmill	E 25.1, 25.2
	Wind motor	E 26.1
	Wind generator farm	E 26.2
	Flagstaff, flagpole	E 27
	Mast	E 28, 30.1

	Radio, television tower	E 29
	Radar scanner	E 30.3
	Dome	E 30.4
	Dish aerial	E 31
	Tank	E 32
	Tank farm	E 32
	Silo	E 33
	Fortified structure	E 34.1
	Fortified structure	E 34.2, 34.3
	Quarry area	E 35.1
	Quarry	E 35.2

F. Ports

Protective Structures		INT/NCC
	Dike as a line	F 1
	Dike as a line, conspicuous	F 1
	Dike as an area	F 1
	Seawall	F 2.1, 2.2
	Causeway as a line	F 3
	Causeway, covers and uncovers as a line	F 3
	Causeway as an area	F 3
	Causeway, covers and uncovers as an area	F 3
	Breakwater or mole as a line	F 4.1-3, 12
	Breakwater or mole as an area	F 4.1-3, 12
	Training wall	F 5
	Groin (always dry)	F 6.1

	Groin (intertidal)	F 6.2
	Groin (submerged)	F 6.3
Harbor Installations		
	Fishing harbor	F 10
	Yacht harbor, marina	F 11.1, 19.2
	Wharf (quay)	F 13
	Pier (jetty), promenade pier	F 14, 15
	Pontoon as a line	F 16
	Pontoon as an area	F16
	Landing	F 17
	Landing steps	F 18
Nr 3	Berth number	F 19.1
	Mooring dolphin	F 20
	Deviation mooring dolphin	F 21
●	Pile or bollard	F 22

	Slipway, ramp	F 23
	Gridiron	F 24
	Dry dock	F 25
	Floating dock as line	F 26
	Floating dock as an area	F 26
	Wet dock and gate	F 27
	Dock	F 28
	Dock, under construction or ruined	F 28
	Floating hazard	F 29.1
	Boom	F 29.1
	Floating oil barrier, oil retention (high pressure pipe)	F 29.1, 29.2
	Boom, floating obstruction	F 29.1

	Ruin or works under construction Year and condition of under construction or ruin is obtained by cursor pick	F 30-33.1
	Pier, ruined and partly submerged	F 33.2
	Hulk	F 34

Canals, Barrages

	Canal	F 40
	Lock gate as a line	F 41.1
	Lock gate as an area	F 41.1
	Navigable lock gate	F 41.2
	Non-navigable lock gate	F 42, 43
	Caisson as a line	F 42
	Caisson as an area	F 42
	Flood barrage as a line	F 43

	Flood barrage as an area	F 43
	Dam as a line	F 44
	Dam as an area	F 44
Transhipment Facilities		
RoRo	RoRo Terminal	F 50
#	Timber yard as a point	F 52
[#]	Timber yard as an area	F 52
⊤	Crane as a point, lifting capacity is obtained by cursor pick	F 53.1-3
	Crane as an area	F 53.1-3
	Crane, visually conspicuous as an area	F 53.1-3
Public Buildings		
⊖	Customs	F 61
■	*[On ENC, public buildings (harbormaster, hospital, post office, etc.) are shown as regular buildings.]*	F 60-63

H. Tides, Currents

Tide Tables		INT/NCC
◇	Point or area for which a tidal stream table is available *[Actual data are not included in U.S. or Canadian ENC.]*	H 31, 46
(ellipse with tidal arrow symbols around ◇)	Boundary of an area for which there is tidal information	H 31, 40, 41
Tidal Streams and Currents		
↑ 2.5 kn	Flood stream, rate at spring tides *[Spring currents are about 20% stronger than average.]*	H 40
? ↑ ?	Current or tidal stream whose direction is not known	H 40, 41
↑ 2.5 kn	Ebb stream, rate at spring tides	H 41
↑ 2.5 kn	Non-tidal current	H 42, 43
⌇⌇⌇	Overfalls, tide rips; eddies; breakers as point *[Cursor pick for important distinctions.]*	H 44, 45
⌇⌇⌇ (dashed line)	Overfalls, tide rips; eddies; breakers as a line	H 44, 45
(⌇⌇⌇) (dashed ellipse)	Overfalls, tide rips; eddies; breakers as an area	H 44, 45

I. Depths

[ENC base units are meters, so U.S. charts with historically native units of feet or fathoms have soundings and depth contours encoded with decimal meters, expressed as subscripts.]

General		INT/NCC
(25)	Sounding of low accuracy, less than or equal to the safety depth.	I 1, 2, 3.1, 4
(25)	Sounding of low accuracy, deeper than the safety depth.	I 2, 4
✖	Hazardous object shallower than the *requested* safety contour located outside of the *displayed* safety contour	I 2, 4
?⟍	Point feature or area of low accuracy	I 3.1, 4
▫ ▫ ▫ ▫ ▫	Low accuracy line demarking area wreck or obstruction	I 3.2
▪ ▪ ▪ ▪ ▪	Low accuracy line demarking foul area	I 3.2
25	Hazardous object less than or equal to the safety depth	
25	Hazardous object deeper than the safety depth	
Soundings *[Color (black or gray) is based on user choice of safety depth.]*		
9₇	Sounding shoaler than or equal to safety depth in decimal meters.	I 10
30	Sounding deeper than safety depth	I 10
Depths are always shown in their true position on ENC.		I 11, 12
(12)	Sounding of low accuracy	I 14

	[Spot drying height (negative soundings) in the foreshore.	I 15
	Tideway	I 16

Depths in Fairways and Areas

	Dredged area Depth, date of latest survey and other information is obtained by cursor pick *[Often shown in named parallel strips, such as LOQ (left outside quadrant) with different control depths.]*	I 20-23
	Swept area	I 24
	Incompletely surveyed area	I 25
	Unsurveyed area	I 25

ENC Portrayal of Depths

ENC depth related symbols closely resemble their paper chart counterparts; but the ENC presentation offers valuable options for additional information to be presented to mariners in an ECS or ECDIS.

Soundings
S-52 standards enables mariners to set their own-ship's *safety depth*. If no safety depth is set, the default value is 30m. Soundings equal to or shoaler than the safety depth are shown in black; deeper soundings are displayed in a less conspicuous gray. Fractional values are shown with subscript numbers of the same size.

Depth Contours and Depth Areas
ENC depth contours are portrayed with a thin gray line. Each pair of adjacent depth contours is used to define a *depth area*. These are used by your ECS or ECDIS to tint different depth levels and to initiate alarms when a ship is headed into unsafe water. *[A 5.4 m (17.7 ft) contour on a NOAA ENC corresponds to the 18 ft contour on the parent RNC.]*

Depth Contour Labels
ENC depth contour labels are not centered and oriented along isolines. They are displayed upright and may appear either on or next to the contour lines they describe. The labels are black and the same size as soundings, but the labels have a light "halo" to set them apart. The graphic shows depth labels and soundings both deeper and shoaler than the safety depth. Because ENC stores depths in meters, soundings and contour lines often show fractional meter values. The *safety contour* (described below) is always displayed, but mariners may choose to have all other depth contours turned off.

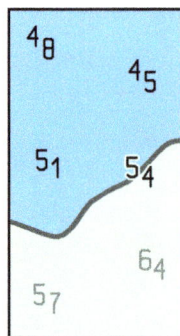

Safety Contour
The S-52 standard calls for the use of a *safety contour* to show an extra thick line for the depth contour that separates *safe water* from shoaler areas. If the mariner does not set an own-ship safety contour value, the default value is 30m. If the ENC being displayed does not have a contour line equal to the safety contour depth value requested by the mariner, then the next deeper contour will be displayed as the safety contour. Depending on the contour intervals used on individual ENC, the displayed safety contour may change as a ship transits from one ENC to another. When own-ships projected position crosses the safety contour an alarm will be displayed.

Two or Four Color Depth Areas

ENC display the color of depth areas beyond the green foreshore in either two or four shades of blue. This is similar to the convention used on paper charts, but the depths used to change colors are based on user-selected contours. If the mariner chooses two shades to be displayed, water deeper than the safety contour is shown in an off-white color, water shoaler than the safety contour is a blue shade.

Two-color depth shading changes at the safety contour

Four-color depth shading changes at user-selected values of a *shallow contour*, the *safety contour*, and a *deep water contour*.

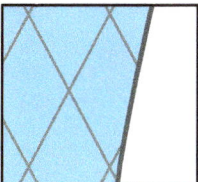

Some ECDIS and ECS also provide the mariner with the option of displaying a cross-hatch shallow-water pattern over all depth areas shoaler than the safety contour.

Depth Contours

	Two Shades	*Four Shades*		
foreshore	(foreshore)	(foreshore)	foreshore	
shallow depth	shallow water contour		very shallow depth	
			medium shallow depth	I 30
	safety contour			
deep depth	deep water contour		medium deep depth	
	all deeper contours		deep depth	

[Contours are shown dashed when of low accuracy.]

▫ ▫ ▫ ▫ ▫	Approximate depth contour	I 31
▫ ▫ ▫ ▫ ▫	Approximate safety contour	I 31

J. Nature of the Seabed

Types of Seabed		INT/NCC
S	Sand *[0.06 mm to 2 mm]*	J 1
M	Mud	J 2
Cy	Clay	J 3
Si	Silt	J 4
St	Stones	J 5
G	Gravel *[2 mm to 4 mm (buckshot to marbles)]*	J 6
P	Pebbles *[4 mm to 64 mm (marbles to golf balls)]*	J 7
Cb	Cobbles *[64 mm to 256 mm (golf to soccer balls)]*	J 8
R	Rock	J 9.1
R	Boulder *[bigger than cobbles]*	J 9.2
R	Lava	J 9.2
Co	Coral	J 10
Sh	Shells	J 11
>>>	Weed, kelp	J 13.1
(>>>)	Weed, kelp as an area	J 13.2
⌃⌃⌃	Sand waves as a point	J 14
⌃⌃⌃	Sand waves as a line	J 14
(⌃⌃⌃)	Sand waves as an area	J 14
⊥	Spring	J 15

Types of Seabed, Intertidal Areas		
	Areas of gravel and stone	J 20
	Rocky ledges or coral reef *[See also I 15.]*	J 21, 22
	[Spot drying heights (negative soundings) in the foreshore]	I 15

ENC Nature of Surface (NATSUR) Definitions

1. **mud:** soft, wet earth.

2. **clay:** (particles of less than 0.002mm); stiff, sticky earth that becomes hard when baked.

3. **silt:** (particles of 0.002 - 0.0625mm); when dried on hand will rub off easily.

4. **sand:** (particles of 0.0625 - 2.0mm); tiny grains of crushed or worn rock.

5. **stone:** a general term for rock fragments ranging in size from pebbles and gravel to boulders or a large rock mass.

6. **gravel:** (particles of 2.0 - 4.0mm); small stones with coarse sand.

7. **pebbles:** (particles of 4.0 - 64.0mm); small stones made smooth and round by being rolled in water.

8. **cobbles:** (particles of 64.0 - 256.0mm); stones worn round and smooth by water and used for paving.

9. **rock:** any formation of natural origin that constitutes an integral part of the lithosphere. The natural occurring material that forms firm, hard, and solid masses.

11. **lava:** the fluid or semi-fluid matter flowing from a volcano. The substance that results from the cooling of the molten rock. Part of the ocean bed is composed of lava.

14. **coral:** hard calcareous skeletons of many tribes of marine polyps.

17. **shells:** exoskeletons of various water dwelling animals.

18. **boulder:** a rounded rock with diameter of 256 mm or larger.

K. Rocks, Wrecks, Obstructions, Aquaculture

Hazards [Rocks, wrecks, and obstructions are often presented as generic hazard symbols.]		INT/NCC
5	Underwater hazard with a sounding less than or equal to the safety depth.	
25	Underwater hazard with a sounding greater than the safety depth	
4	Underwater hazard that covers and uncovers with known drying height *[See also Section I. Depths.]*	K 11, 12
	Underwater hazard that covers and uncovers	K 12
✖	Isolated danger with depth less than the *requested* safety contour	

Rocks [Cursor pick all rocks you may encounter for full details.]		
✳	Rock that covers and uncovers or is awash at low water	K 11, 12
⊕	Dangerous underwater rock of uncertain depth	K 13, 16
5 25	Hazard symbols can be rocks. Cursor pick to determine. Color depends on safety depth	K 11, 13, 14.1, 14.2, 15; O 27
✖	Isolated danger symbol could be a rock. Cursor pick to determine.	
●	Land as a point at small scale	K 10

Wrecks		
	Wreck showing any portion of hull or superstructure at level of chart datum *[Chart datum means zero tide height]*	K 24, 25
	Dangerous wreck, depth unknown	K 28
	Non-dangerous wreck, depth unknown	K 29
	Hazard symbols can be wrecks. Cursor pick to determine. Color depends on safety depth	K 6, 27, 30
	Isolated danger symbol could be a wreck. Cursor pick to determine.	
Obstructions		
	Obstruction, depth not stated	K 1, 16, 40, 43
	Obstruction with known depth	
	Obstruction that covers and uncovers	K 1
	Fish Haven	K 46.1
#	Foul area of seabed safe for navigation but not for anchoring	K 31.1, 31.2
	Hazard symbols can be obstructions. Cursor pick to determine. Color depends on safety depth	I 2, 4; K 1, 16, 40, 41, 42, 46.2; L 20, 21.2, 43; Q 42
	Isolated danger symbol could be an obstruction. Cursor pick to determine.	
Aquaculture		
	Fish stakes as a point	K 44.1
	Fish stakes as an area	K 44.1

	Fish trap, fish weir, tunny net as a point	K 44.2
	Fish trap, fish weir, tunny net as an area	K 45
	Marine farm as a point	K 47
	Marine farm as an area	K 48.1, 48.2
General		
	Safe clearance shoaler than safety contour	K 16, 40, 46.1, 46.2
12_8	Safe clearance deeper than safety contour	K 16
25_6	Safe clearance deeper than the safety depth	K 16, 46.2
	Foul area, not safe for navigation	K 1
#	Foul ground	K 31.1, 31.2
	Distributed remains of wreck	K 31.1, 31.2
4	Swept sounding, less than or equal to safety depth	K 2
21	Swept sounding, greater than safety depth	K 2

L. Offshore Installations

General		INT/NCC
	Area where entry is prohibited or restricted or to be avoided, with other cautions	L 3
	Cautionary area, navigate with caution Wind farm (offshore) Wave farm	L 4, 5.2, 6
	Wind motor visually conspicuous	L 5.1
Platforms and Moorings		
	Offshore platform	L 10, 17, 2, 12-15
	Conspicuous flare stack on offshore platform	L 11
	Installation buoy and mooring buoy, simplified	L 16
	Installation buoy, paper chart	L 16
	Ground tackle	L 18
Underwater Installations		
	Underwater hazard with depth less than or equal to the safety depth	L 20, 21.2
	Underwater hazard with depth greater than the safety depth	L 20, 21.2
	Isolated danger of depth less than the requested safety contour	L 20, 21.1-3
	Foul area of seabed safe for navigation but not for anchoring	L 22
	Obstruction in the water which is always above water level	L 23

	Underwater turbine or subsurface ODAS	L 24
	Underwater turbine or subsurface ODAS	L 25

Submarine Cables

	Submarine cable, status is obtained by cursor pick	L 30.1, 30.2, 32
	Submarine cable area	L 31.1, 31.2

Submarine Pipelines

	Oil, gas pipeline, submerged or on land	L 40.1
	Submarine pipeline area with potentially dangerous contents	L 40.2
	Water pipeline, sewer, etc.	L 41.1
	Submarine pipeline area with generally non-dangerous contents	L 41.2
	Pipeline tunnel	L 42.2
	Underwater hazard with depth less than or equal to the safety depth	L 43
	Isolated danger of depth less than the requested safety contour	L 43

M. Tracks, Routes

Tracks		INT/NCC
Leading line bearing a non-regulated, recommended track		
-<?>− − −<	Direction not encoded	M 1
270 deg	One-way	M 1
270 deg	Two-way	M 1
270 deg	Clearing line; transit line	M 2
Non-regulated, recommended track based on fixed marks		
-<?>− − −<	Direction not encoded	M 3, 32.2
90 deg	One-way	M 3, 32.2
270 deg	Two-way	M 3, 32.2
Non-regulated, recommended track not based on fixed marks		
-<?>− − −<	Direction not encoded	M 4
90 deg	One-way	M 4
270 deg	Two-way	M 4
Based on fixed marks, one-way		
90 deg	Non-regulated recommended track	M 5.1
→— DW —→	Deep water route	M 5.1
Not based on fixed marks, one-way		
90 deg	Non-regulated recommended track	M 5.2
—>— D_W —	Deep water route centerline	M 5.2

Routing Measures		
➡	Traffic direction in a one-way lane of a traffic separation scheme	M 10
⊏==▷	Single traffic direction in a two-way route part of a traffic separation scheme	M 11
	Traffic separation line	M 12
	Traffic separation zone	M 13
— — — — —	Traffic separation scheme boundary	M 15
⚠	Traffic precautionary area as a point	M 16
	Traffic precautionary area as an area *[Cross-hatching and border symbols only appear when symbolized display is chosen.]*	M 16
	Axis and boundary of archipelagic sea lane	M 17
	Fairway, depth is obtained by cursor pick	M 18
Radar Surveillance Systems		
◉	Radar station	M 30
	Radar range	M 31
— — 270 deg — —	Radar line	M 32.1

43

Radio Reporting Points

Nr 13 ch s74	Radio calling-in point for traffic in one direction only	M 40.1
Nr 13 ch s74	Radio calling-in point for traffic in both directions	M 40.1
? ? Nr 13 ch s74	Radio calling-in point, direction not encoded	M 40.1
Nr 13 ch s74	Radio calling-in point for traffic in one direction only	M 40.2
Nr 13 ch s74	Radio calling-in point for traffic in both directions	M 40.2
Nr 13 ? ? ch s74	Radio calling-in point, direction not encoded	M 40.2

Ferries

	Ferry route	M 50
	Cable ferry route	M 51

Routing Objects *[Displayed on the following diagram.]*	
(18)	Safety fairway
(20.1)	Traffic Separation Scheme (TSS), traffic separated by separation zone
(20.2)	Traffic Separation Scheme, traffic separated by natural obstructions
(20.3)	Traffic Separation Scheme, with outer separation zone separating traffic using scheme from traffic not using it
(21)	Traffic Separation Scheme, roundabout with separation zone
(22)	Traffic Separation Scheme, with "crossing gates"
(23)	Traffic Separation Scheme crossing, without designated precautionary area
(24)	Precautionary area
(25.1)	Inshore Traffic Zone (ITZ), with defined end limits
(25.2)	Inshore Traffic Zone, without defined end limits
(26.1)	Recommended direction of traffic flow, between traffic separation schemes
(26.2)	Recommended direction of traffic flow,
(27.1)	Deep Water Route (DW), as part of a one-way traffic lane
(27.2)	Two-way deep water route, with minimum depth stated
(27.3)	Deep water route, centerline as recommended one-way or two-way track
(28.1)	Recommended route, one-way and two-way (often marked by centerline buoys)
(28.2)	Two-way route, with one-way sections
(29.1)	Area to be Avoided (ATBA), around navigational aid
(29.2)	Area to be Avoided, e.g. because of danger of stranding

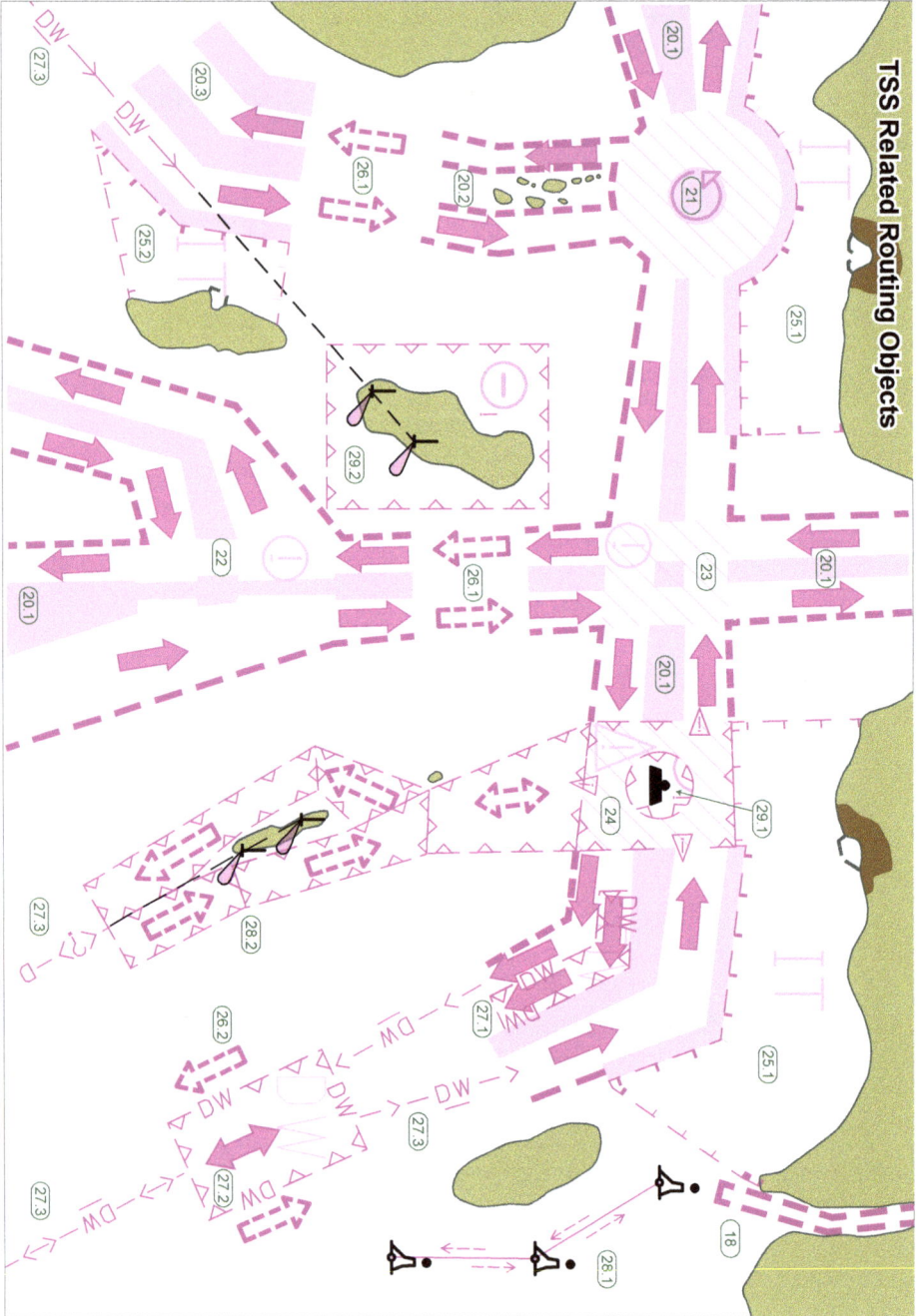

TSS Related Routing Objects

[See object key on the previous page.]

N. Areas, Limits

[Important chart notes on Areas are found by cursor pick. Land areas and regions are considered Natural and Cultural Features.]

[The identifier symbols shown inside the areas of this section move on the screen to stay near the center of the viewed areas they define. They are called self-centering symbols.]

General	INT/NCC
ENC represent many types of area limits with just a few different symbols. Information about the type of area and its associated restrictions or prohibitions may be obtained by cursor pick.	
Caution area, a specific caution note applies *[The line decorations on all ENC defined areas point into the area being defined, which is valuable to know when just a segment of the border is in view.]*	N 1.1, 1.2
Area where entry is prohibited or restricted or to be avoided *[An "i", if present means additional information is available; an "!" means other cautions apply.]*	N 2.1, 2.2
Anchorages, Anchorage Areas	
Anchorage area as a point at small scale, or anchor points of mooring trot at large scale	N 10
Anchor berth	N 11.1
Type of anchorage area is obtained by cursor pick	N 12.1-9

Note: Anchors as part of the limit symbol are not shown for small areas. Other types of anchorage areas may be shown.		
	Seaplane landing area	N 13

Restricted Areas

	Area where anchoring is prohibited or restricted *[An "i", if present, means additional information is available; an "!" means other cautions apply.]*	N 20
	Area where fishing or trawling is prohibited or restricted *[An "i", if present, means additional information is available; an "!" means other cautions apply.]*	N 21.1
	Area where diving is prohibited	N 21.2
ESSA	Environmentally Sensitive Sea Area (ESSA)	N 22.1-3
	Area with minor restrictions or information notices	N 22.1-3
PSSA	Particularly Sensitive Sea Area (PSSA)	N 22.4
	Explosives or chemical dumping ground as a point	N 23.1

	Explosives or chemical dumping ground as an area	N 23.2, 24
	Degaussing area	N 25

Military Practice Areas

	Restricted area	N 30, 32, 33
	Area where entry is prohibited or restricted or to be avoided, with other cautions. Minefield	N 31, 34

International Boundaries and National Limits

	Jurisdiction boundary	N 40, 41
	Straight territorial sea baseline, Custom regulation zone	N 42, 48
	Territorial sea, Contiguous zone, Limits of fishery zone, Continental shelf area, Exclusive economic zone	N 43-47
	Harbor area, symbolized	N 49

Various Limits

	Continuous pattern for an ice area (glacier, etc.)	N 60.1, 60.2
	Floating hazard	N 61

	Boom, ice boom	N 61
	Boom, ice boom, floating obstruction, log pond	N 61
	HO information note	N 62.1, 62.2, 64, 65
	Dredging area	N 63
	Area of specified Compilation scale (M_CSCL) or Area of specified ENC coverage (M_COVR)	
	Area of specified Category of Zone of Confidence	

P. Lights

[Typical attributes of lights include: category, color, characteristic, group, period, sectors, nominal range, height, name, exhibition condition, multiplicity, name, system of navigational marks, among others. Lights can be located on buoys, beacons, landmarks, or single buildings.]

Light Structures and Major Floating Lights		INT/NCC
	Light, lighthouse, paper chart	P 1
	Light, lighthouse, paper chart	P 1
	Lighted offshore platform, paper chart	P 2
	Lighted beacon tower, paper chart	P 3

	Lighted beacon, paper chart	P 4, 5
	Light vessel, paper chart	P 6

Light Characters

	When text for lights is displayed, ENC use INT abbreviations.	P 10.1-11, 12-14
	Default light symbol if no color is encoded or color is other than red, green, white, yellow, amber, or orange	P 11.1-8
	Red	P 11.1-8
	Green	P 11.1-8
	White, yellow, amber or orange	P 11.1-8
	Sector Lights *[Sector lights do not include characteristic labels.]*	P 11.1-8

Example of a Full Light Descriptions

	The descriptions of non-sector lights are shown on ENC when the display of text is turned on, as shown. (The aid to navigation or other structure that is always shown attached to the ENC light symbols are not depicted here.) *[Lights with nominal range < 10 nmi are flares; brighter lights are usually rings, but some ECS have the option to use or not use the rings.]*	P 16

Fl R 15s 21m 6M

Fl G 10s 15m 11M

Lights Marking Fairways

	Leading lights with sectors	P 20.1
	Leading lights	P 20.2
	Lights in line, marking the sides of a channel	P 21

Direction Lights

	Directional light with sector	P30.1
	Directional light without sector	P 30.2
	Light, directional	P 30.3, 30.4
	Category of light as moiré effect is obtained by cursor pick	P 31

Sector Lights *[Sector lights do not include characteristic labels.]*		
	Light, sector	P 40.1, 40.2
	Light, danger	P 42
	Light, obscured *[Obscured lights are considered Sector lights and thus do not include characteristic labels.]*	P 43
	Light, restricted	P 44
	Light, faint	P 45
	Light, intensified	P 46
Special Lights		
AeroAlFlWG7.5s11M	Light	P 60
AeroFR313m11M	Conspicuous mast with light	P 61.1, 61.2
O≡	Floodlight	P 63
/W	Strip light	P 64

"Paper Chart" and Simplified Symbols

ENC can be set to display aids to navigation with what they call "paper chart" symbols or "simplified symbols." The two symbol sets are shown here. Some ECDIS and ECS color fill the paper chart buoy shapes, but this is not required by IHO S-52 specifications.

[Simplified cardinal buoy symbols have an IHO specified outline thickness that is twice that of cardinal beacons, but individual ECS or ECDIS displays may not reflect this.]

[On both paper charts and ENC displays, floating objects are tilted, whereas fixed beacons are shown vertical—a convention that helps interpret the symbols. Even the labels are tilted (italics) to support the convention.]

Floating Marks		
Paper Chart	Simplified	Simplified Symbol name
▲*	◿	Cardinal buoy, north
◆*	◹	Cardinal buoy, east
▼*	◺	Cardinal buoy, south
⋈*	◹	Cardinal buoy, west
⚲?	◉ ?	Default symbol for buoy (used when no defining attributes have been encoded in the ENC)
⦂*	⦂	Isolated danger buoy
⌂	◿◹	Conical lateral buoy, green or red
⌂	◿◹	Pillar lateral buoy, green or red
⌁	◇	Can shape lateral buoy, green
⌁	◇	Can shape lateral buoy, red
⌂ ⌂ ⌂	♣	Installation buoy and mooring buoy

**	🔴	Safe water buoy
⬭	🟡	Special purpose buoy, spherical or barrel shaped, or default symbol for special purpose buoy
⬭	◁	Special purpose TSS buoy marking the starboard side of the traffic lane
⬭	▱	Special purpose TSS buoy marking the port side of the traffic lane
⬭ ⌇	⁄	Special purpose ice buoy or spar shaped buoy
⬭	▬	Super-buoy ODAS & LANBY
⬭	⬗	Light float
⬭	⬗	Light vessel

Fixed Marks

Paper Chart	Simplified	Simplified Symbol name
▲	⟁	Cardinal beacon, north
◆	⬙	Cardinal beacon, east
▼	▽	Cardinal beacon, south
⋈	⋈	Cardinal beacon, west
⌇?	▯?	Default symbol for beacon (used when no defining attributes have been encoded in the ENC)
⊥	▮	Isolated danger beacon
	▮	Major lateral beacon, red
⌇	▮	Major lateral beacon, green
	▮	Minor lateral beacon, green

* Paper chart symbols display various buoy or beacon shape symbols in conjunction with the topmark.

** Several different paper chart symbols correspond to this simplified symbol

⬡	▮	Major safe water beacon *[Major beacon symbols are used for tower, lattice, and pile beacons, specified in the attribute Beacon shape.]*
	▮	Minor safe water beacon
⬡	▯	Major special purpose beacon
	▯	Minor special purpose beacon

Day Marks

Paper Chart	Simplified	Simplified Symbol name
⬛	⬛	Square or rectangular daymark
△	△	Triangular daymark, point up
▽	▽	Triangular daymark, point down
⩲	⩲	Retro Reflector

Q. Buoys, Beacons

[Typical Attributes of Buoys and Beacons: Shape, Color, Color pattern, Con-dition, Radar conspicuous, Visually conspicuous, Height, System of naviga-tional marks, Nature of construction, and Object name, among others.]

Buoys and Beacons		INT/NCC
⚲?	Default symbol for buoy, paper chart	
●?	Default symbol for buoy, simplified	

⬇?	Default symbol for a beacon, paper chart	
▯?	Default symbol for a beacon, simplified	
ENC show the position of buoys and beacons with a circle at the bottom of paper chart symbols. For simplified symbols, the position of the aid corresponds with the center of the symbol.		Q 1

Colors of Buoys and Beacon Topmarks

⊨	Retro reflector	Q 6

Topmarks and Radar Reflectors*

Paper chart symbols for topmarks are always displayed above a buoy or beacon shape symbol, as in Q 10 and Q 11. Simplified symbols for cardinal marks, isolated dangers, and safe water, consist of only the topmark without the buoy shape symbol. Simplified symbology for marks with any other type of topmark will display on the simplified buoy or beacon shape symbol without a topmark.

Paper Chart	Simplified		
▲▲	◢◢	2 cones point upward *[Cardinal mark, North]*	Q 9
▲▼	◢▽	2 cones base to base *[Cardinal mark, East]*	Q 9
▼▼	▽▽	2 cones point downward *[Cardinal mark, South]*	Q 9
▼▲	▽◢	2 cones point to point *[Cardinal mark, West]*	Q 9
●●	∘∘	2 spheres *[Isolated danger]*	Q 9
●	⊙	Sphere *[Safewater]*	Q 9
▲		Cone point up	Q 9
▼		Cone point down	Q 9
▯		Cylinder, square, vertical rectangle	Q 9
✗		X-shape	Q 9
/		Flag or other shape	Q 9
▭		Board, horizontal rectangle	Q 9

◇		Cube point up	Q 9
┼		Upright cross over a circle	Q 9
⊤		T-shape	Q 9
bn No 2 ⌷		Beacon in general with topmark, paper chart	Q 10
by No 3 △		Conical buoy with topmark, paper chart	Q 11

*ENC do not display labels for radar reflectors on fixed or floating aids; this information is obtained by cursor pick.

Shapes of Buoys

Paper Chart	Simplified		
⌂	◢ ◢	Conical buoy	Q 20
⊏⊐	▱ ▱	Can buoy	Q 21
⌂	⊙	Spherical buoy	Q 22
⌂	◢ ◢	Pillar Buoy	Q 23
↓	⫽	Spar Buoy	Q 24
⌂	⊙	Barrel Buoy	Q 25
⌂		Super-buoy	Q 26
⌂*		Lanby, super-buoy	Q 26
	◤	Super-buoy odas & lanby	Q 26

Minor Light Floats

Paper Chart	Simplified		
⛴	⛴	Light float	Q 30
⛴	⛴	Light float	Q 31

Mooring Buoys

	Mooring buoy, can shape, paper chart	Q 40
	Mooring buoy, barrel shape, paper chart	Q 40
	Installation buoy and mooring buoy, simplified	Q 40
	Mooring buoy with light flare, barrel shape, paper chart	Q 41
Nr 1	Trot, mooring buoys with ground tackle and berth numbers	Q 42
	[Buoys with submarine cables show this symbol. Cursor pick for details.]	Q 43
	Small craft mooring area	Q 44
	Availability of visitor moorings at marina is obtained by cursor pick	Q 45

Special Purpose Buoys

	Conical buoy with topmark, paper chart	Q 50-57, 59, 62
	Special purpose buoy, spherical or barrel shaped, or default symbol for special purpose buoy, simplified	Q 50-59
	Super-buoy, paper chart	Q 58

	Super-buoy odas & lanby simplified	Q 58
	Spherical buoy, paper chart	Q 58
	Conical buoy, paper chart	Q 60
Beacons		
	Default symbol for a beacon, paper chart	Q 80
	Default symbol for a beacon, simplified	Q 80
	Beacon in general, paper chart	Q 80
	Beacon in general with topmark, paper chart	Q 82
	Major red lateral beacon, simplified	Q 82
	Beacon in general with topmark, paper chart	Q 82
	Cardinal beacon, north, simplified	Q 82
	Beacon in general with topmark, paper chart	Q 82, 83
	Isolated danger beacon, simplified	Q 82, 83
Minor Impermanent Marks Usually in Drying Areas (Lateral Marks of Minor Channels)		
	Minor, stake or pole beacon, paper chart	Q 90-92
	Minor red lateral beacon, simplified	Q 91, 92
	Minor green lateral beacon, simplified	Q 91, 92

Minor Marks, Usually on Land		
♣	Conspicuous cairn	Q 100
	Square or rectangular day mark, paper chart	Q 101
	Square or rectangular day mark, simplified	Q 101
	Triangular day mark, point up, paper chart	Q 101
	Triangular day mark, point up, simplified	Q 101
	Triangular day mark, point down, paper chart	Q 101
	Triangular day mark, point down, simplified	Q 101

Beacon Towers		
	Beacon tower, paper chart	Q 110
	Beacon tower with topmarks, paper chart	Q 110
	Major red lateral beacon, simplified	Q 110
	Major green lateral beacon, simplified	Q 110
	Lattice beacon, paper chart	Q 111

Special Purpose Beacons		
270 deg	Leading beacons	Q 120
270 deg	Beacons marking a clearing line or transit	Q 121

	Beacons marking measured distance	Q 122
	[Beacons with submarine cables show this symbol. Cursor pick for details.] Cable landing beacon (example)	Q 123
	Notice board	Q 126

Direction of Buoyage		
The direction of buoyage is that taken when approaching a harbor from seaward. Along coasts, the direction is determined by buoyage authorities, normally clockwise around land masses.		
Symbols showing direction of buoyage where it is not obvious		
	General symbol for direction of buoyage *[Inside symbols are self-centering.]*	Q 130.2
	IALA Region A	Q 130.2
	IALA Region B	Q 130.2

62

Cardinal Marks

Indicating navigable water to the named side of the marks. In the illustration below all marks are the same in Regions A and B.

	Paper chart symbology	Q 130.3
	Simplified symbology	Q 130.3

Isolated Danger Marks

Stationed over dangers with navigable water around them.

	Pillar buoy with 2 spheres topmark	Q 130.4
	Spar buoy with 2 spheres topmark	Q 130.4
	Isolated danger buoy, simplified	Q 130.4

Safe Water Marks		
Such as mid-channel and landfall marks.		
	Spherical buoy, paper chart	Q 130.5
	Pillar buoy with sphere topmark	Q 130.5
	Spar buoy with sphere topmark	Q 130.5
	Safe water buoy, simplified	Q 130.5
Special Marks		
Not primarily to assist navigation but to indicate special features.		
	Spherical buoy, paper chart	Q 130.5
	Can buoy	Q 130.6
	Conical buoy	Q 130.6
	Spar buoy with x-shape topmark	Q 130.6
	Special purpose buoy, simplified	Q 130.6
New Danger Marks		
	Pillar Buoy with upright cross topmark Pillar Buoy with upright cross topmark	Q 130.7

R. Fog Signals

General		INT/NCC
⊙	Position of a conspicuous point feature with fog signal	R 1
	Lighted pillar buoy, paper chart with fog signal	R 1
	Lighted super-buoy, paper chart with fog signal	R 1

Examples of Fog Signal Descriptions		
Note: The fog signal symbol will usually be omitted when a description of the signal is given.		
	Light with fog signal	R 20
	Pillar buoy, paper chart with fog signal	R 21

Paper Chart	Simplified		
		Lighted pillar buoy, with fog signal	R 22

S. Radar, Radio, Satellite Navigation Systems

Radar			INT/NCC
	◯		Radar station *[The S-52 explanation of this symbol is "Radio Station" but it is used to depict both radio stations and radar stations. Use cursor pick.]*	S 1
	◌		Radar transponder beacon	S 2, S 3.1-5
Paper Chart	Simplified		
⟨⚓⟩	⟨⬚⟩		Radar transponder on floating mark	S 3.6
	☼		Symbol indicating this object is radar conspicuous	S 4, S 5
Radio			
	◯		Radio station	S 10-16

Additional information regarding radio, such as category of radio station, signal frequency, communication channel, call sign, estimated signal range, periodicity and status may be included in the cursor pick.

The presence of an AIS transmitted signal intended for use as an aid to navigation associated with a physical aid, including the AIS MMSI Number, can be obtained by cursor pick on the physical aid.

△ V-AIS	North cardinal virtual aid	
◇ V-AIS	East cardinal virtual aid	S 18.2
▽ V-AIS	South cardinal virtual aid	
⋈ V-AIS	West cardinal virtual aid	
▱ V-AIS	Port Lateral (IALA B) virtual aid	S 18.3
◺ V-AIS	Starboard Lateral (IALA B) virtual aid	
⦿ V-AIS	Isolated Danger virtual aid	S 18.4
⦿ V-AIS	Safe Water virtual aid	S 18.5
⦿ V-AIS	Special Purpose virtual aid	S 18.6
⦿ V-AIS	Emergency Wreck virtual aid	S 18.7

Satellite Navigation Systems

◯ DGPS	DGPS reference station	S 51

T. Services

Pilotage		INT/NCC
◈	Pilot boarding place	T 1.1-4
◈	Pilot boarding area	T 1.1-4
Coast Guard, Rescue		
CG	Coast Guard station	T 10, T 11
◆	Rescue station	T 11-14
Signal Stations		
SS	Signal station	T 20-36

APPENDIX
ENC Objects and Attributes

Refer to notes in the Preface about the role of ENC objects and attributes and a link to a valuable online catalog that defines each of them. Both ECDIS and ECS have differing policies and options about the use of the acronyms in the cursor pick reports. In some cases they are clearly valuable for communication, in other cases, less so. The IHO discourages their use.

How NOAA presents ENC pick reports can be seen using their online interactive ENC viewer at

www.nauticalcharts.noaa.gov/enconline/enconline.html

NOAA uses acronyms in their reports, so this Appendix can help translate them, or use the online object catalog. Below is a sample of an extended pick report from a different ECS that does not use acronyms.

A pick report starts with the chart name and location picked, then lists all objects at the location along with their associated attributes. Often there is detailed information such as the light sequence (i.e., 0.3s flash with 2.2s off), often valuable with complex lights. The Dredged area picked is the left outside quadrant (LOQ), which we learn from its name, with the implication that other quadrants could have other control depths.

The NOAA paper chart of this region (12256) was permanently canceled on 3/6/24.

US5VA20M

36° 58.260' N, 076° 06.297' W

Buoy, lateral

Shape	Pillar
Category	Port-hand lateral mark
Color	Green
Name	Thimble Shoal Channel Lighted Buoy 7

Light

Color	Green
Exhibition condition	Night light
Characteristic	Flashing
Group	(1)
Period	2.5 s
Sequence	00.3+(02.2)

Fairway

Name	Thimble Shoal Channel
Traffic	Two-way

Magnetic variation

Reference year	2015
Annual change	-1'
Variation	-11°

Depth area

Contours	10.9 m - 36.5 m

Dredged area

Sounding	14.5 m
Name	Thimble Shoal Channel LOQ

OBJECT	ACRONYM	OBJECT	ACRONYM
Administration Area	ADMARE	Current - non-gravitational	CURENT
Airport/airfield	AIRARE	Custom zone	CUSZNE
Anchor berth	ACHBRT	Dam	DAMCON
Archipelagic Sea Lane	ARCSLN	Daymark	DAYMAR
Archipelagic Sea Lane Axis	ASLXIS	Deep water route centerline	DWRTCL
Anchorage area	ACHARE	Deep water route part	DWRTPT
Beacon, cardinal	BCNCAR	Depth area	DEPARE
Beacon, isolated danger	BCNISD	Depth contour	DEPCNT
Beacon, lateral	BCNLAT	Distance mark	DISMAR
Beacon, safe water	BCNSAW	Dock area	DOCARE
Beacon, special purpose/ general	BCNSPP	Dredged area	DRGARE
		Dry dock	DRYDOC
Berth	BERTHS	Dumping ground	DMPGRD
Bridge	BRIDGE	Dyke	DYKCON
Building, single	BUISGL	Exclusive economic zone	EXEZNE
Built-up area	BUAARE	Fairway	FAIRWY
Buoy, cardinal	BOYCAR	Fence/wall	FNCLNE
Buoy, installation	BOYINB	Ferry route	FERYRT
Buoy, isolated danger	BOYISD	Fishery zone	FSHZNE
Buoy, lateral	BOYLAT	Fishing facility	FSHFAC
Buoy, safe water	BOYSAW	Fishing ground	FSHGRD
Buoy, special purpose/ general	BOYSPP	Floating dock	FLODOC
		Fog signal	FOGSIG
Cable area	CBLARE	Fortified structure	FORSTC
Cable, overhead	CBLOHD	Free port area	FRPARE
Cable, submarine	CBLSUB	Gate	GATCON
Canal	CANALS	Gridiron	GRIDRN
Cargo transhipment area	CTSARE	Harbour area (administrative)	HRBARE
Causeway	CAUSWY		
Caution area	CTNARE	Harbour facility	HRBFAC
Checkpoint	CHKPNT	Hulk	HULKES
Coastguard station	CGUSTA	Ice area	ICEARE
Coastline	COALNE	Incineration area	ICNARE
Contiguous zone	CONZNE	Inshore traffic zone	ISTZNE
Continental shelf area	COSARE	Lake	LAKARE
Control point	CTRPNT	Land area	LNDARE
Conveyor	CONVYR	Land elevation	LNDELV
Crane	CRANES	Land region	LNDRGN

OBJECT	ACRONYM	OBJECT	ACRONYM
Landmark	LNDMRK	Recommended track	RECTRC
Light	LIGHTS	Recommended traffic lane part	RCTLPT
Light float	LITFLT		
Light vessel	LITVES	Rescue station	RSCSTA
Local magnetic anomaly	LOCMAG	Restricted area	RESARE
Lock basin	LOKBSN	Retro-reflector	RETRFL
Log pond	LOGPON	River	RIVERS
Magnetic variation	MAGVAR	Road	ROADWY
Marine farm/culture	MARCUL	Runway	RUNWAY
Military practice area	MIPARE	Sand waves	SNDWAV
Mooring/Warping facility	MORFAC	Sea area/named water area	SEAARE
Navigation line	NAVLNE	Sea-plane landing area	SPLARE
New object	NEWOBJ	Seabed area	SBDARE
Obstruction	OBSTRN	Shoreline construction	SLCONS
Offshore platform	OFSPLF	Signal station, traffic	SISTAT
Offshore production area	OSPARE	Signal station, warning	SISTAW
Oil barrier	OILBAR	Silo/tank	SILTNK
Pile	PILPNT	Slope topline	SLOTOP
Pilot boarding place	PILBOP	Sloping ground	SLOGRD
Pipeline area	PIPARE	Small craft facility	SMCFAC
Pipeline, overhead	PIPOHD	Sounding	SOUNDG
Pipeline, submarine/on land	PIPSOL	Spring	SPRING
Pontoon	PONTON	Straight territorial sea baseline	STSLNE
Precautionary area	PRCARE	Submarine transit lane	SUBTLN
Production/storage area	PRDARE	Swept Area	SWPARE
Pylon/bridge support	PYLONS	Territorial sea area	TESARE
Radar line	RADLNE	Tidal stream - flood/ebb	TS_FEB
Radar range	RADRNG	Tidal stream - harmonic prediction	TS_PRH
Radar reflector	RADRFL		
Radar station	RADSTA	Tidal stream - non-harmonic prediction	TS_PNH
Radar transponder beacon	RTPBCN		
Radio calling-in point	RDOCAL	Tidal stream panel data	TS_PAD
Radio station	RDOSTA	Tidal stream - time series	TS_TIS
Railway	RAILWY	Tide - harmonic prediction	T_HMON
Rapids	RAPIDS	Tide - non-harmonic pre-diction	T_NHMN
Recommended route cen-terline	RCRTCL		
		Tide - time series	T_TIMS

Electronic Chart Symbols

OBJECT	ACRONYM	OBJECT	ACRONYM
Tideway	TIDEWY	Waterfall	WATFAL
Topmark	TOPMAR	Weed/Kelp	WEDKLP
Traffic separation line	TSELNE	Wreck	WRECKS
Traffic separation scheme boundary	TSSBND	Accuracy of data	M_ACCY
		Compilation scale of data	M_CSCL
Traffic separation scheme crossing	TSSCRS	Coverage	M_COVR
Traffic separation scheme lane part	TSSLPT	Horizontal datum shift parameters	M_HOPA
Traffic separation scheme roundabout	TSSRON	Nautical publication information	M_NPUB
Traffic separation zone	TSEZNE	Navigational system of marks	M_NSYS
Tunnel	TUNNEL	Quality of data	M_QUAL
Two-way route part	TWRTPT	Sounding datum	M_SDAT
Underwater/awash rock	UWTROC	Survey reliability	M_SREL
Unsurveyed area	UNSARE	Vertical datum of data	M_VDAT
Vegetation	VEGATN	Aggregation	C_AGGR
Water turbulence	WATTUR	Association	C_ASSO

ATTRIBUTE	ACRONYM	ATTRIBUTE	ACRONYM
Agency responsible for production	AGENCY	Category of control point	CATCTR
		Category of conveyor	CATCON
Beacon shape	BCNSHP	Category of coverage	CATCOV
Building shape	BUISHP	Category of crane	CATCRN
Buoy shape	BOYSHP	Category of dam	CATDAM
Buried depth	BURDEP	Category of distance mark	CATDIS
Call sign	CALSGN	Category of dock	CATDOC
Category of airport/airfield	CATAIR	Category of dumping ground	CATDPG
Category of anchorage	CATACH		
Category of bridge	CATBRG	Category of fenceline	CATFNC
Category of built-up area	CATBUA	Category of ferry	CATFRY
Category of cable	CATCBL	Category of fishing facility	CATFIF
Category of canal	CATCAN	Category of fog signal	CATFOG
Category of cardinal mark	CATCAM	Category of fortified structure	CATFOR
Category of checkpoint	CATCHP		
Category of coastline	CATCOA	Category of gate	CATGAT

ATTRIBUTE	ACRONYM	ATTRIBUTE	ACRONYM
Category of ice	CATICE	Category of shoreline construction	CATSLC
Category of installation buoy	CATINB	Category of signal station, traffic	CATSIT
Category of land region	CATLND	Category of signal station, warning	CATSIW
Category of landmark	CATLMK	Category of silo/tank	CATSIL
Category of lateral mark	CATLAM	Category of slope	CATSLO
Category of light	CATLIT	Category of small craft facility	CATSCF
Category of marine farm/culture	CATMFA	Category of special purpose mark	CATSPM
Category of military practice area	CATMPA	Category of Tidal Stream	CAT_TS
Category of mooring/warping facility	CATMOR	Category of Traffic Separation Scheme	CATTSS
Category of obstruction	CATOBS	Category of vegetation	CATVEG
Category of offshore platform	CATOFP	Category of water turbulence	CATWAT
Category of oil barrier	CATOLB	Category of weed/kelp	CATWED
Category of pile	CATPLE	Category of wreck	CATWRK
Category of pilot boarding place	CATPIL	Category of zone of confidence in data	CATZOC
Category of pipeline/pipe	CATPIP	Character spacing	$SPACE
Category of production area	CATPRA	Character specification	$CHARS
Category of pylon	CATPYL	Colour	COLOUR
Category of quality of data	CATQUA	Colour pattern	COLPAT
Category of radar station	CATRAS	Communication channel	COMCHA
Category of radar transponder beacon	CATRTB	Compass size	$CSIZE
Category of radio station	CATROS	Compilation date	CPDATE
Category of recommended track	CATTRK	Compilation scale	CSCALE
Category of rescue station	CATRSC	Condition	CONDTN
Category of restricted area	CATREA	Conspicuous, radar	CONRAD
Category of road	CATROD	Conspicuous, visually	CONVIS
Category of runway	CATRUN	Current velocity	CURVEL
Category of sea area	CATSEA	Date end	DATEND
		Date start	DATSTA
		Depth range value 1	DRVAL1

73

Electronic Chart Symbols

ATTRIBUTE	ACRONYM	ATTRIBUTE	ACRONYM
Depth range value 2	DRVAL2	Pictorial representation	PICREP
Depth units	DUNITS	Pilot district	PILDST
Elevation	ELEVAT	Positional accuracy units	PUNITS
Estimated range of transmission	ESTRNG	Producing country	PRCTRY
		Product	PRODCT
Exhibition condition of light	EXCLIT	Publication reference	PUBREF
Exposition of sounding	EXPSOU	Quality of sounding measurement	QUASOU
Function	FUNCTN		
Height	HEIGHT	Radar wave length	RADWAL
Height/length units	HUNITS	Radius	RADIUS
Horizontal accuracy	HORACC	Recording date	RECDAT
Horizontal clearance	HORCLR	Recording indication	RECIND
Horizontal length	HORLEN	Reference year for magnetic variation	RYRMGV
Horizontal width	HORWID		
Ice factor	ICEFAC	Restriction	RESTRN
Information	INFORM	Scale maximum	SCAMAX
Jurisdiction	JRSDTN	Scale minimum	SCAMIN
Justification - horizontal	$JUSTH	Scale value one	SCVAL1
Justification - vertical	$JUSTV	Scale value two	SCVAL2
Lifting capacity	LIFCAP	Sector limit one	SECTR1
Light characteristic	LITCHR	Sector limit two	SECTR2
Light visibility	LITVIS	Shift parameters	SHIPAM
Marks navigational - System of	MARSYS	Signal frequency	SIGFRQ
		Signal generation	SIGGEN
Multiplicity of lights	MLTYLT	Signal group	SIGGRP
Nationality	NATION	Signal period	SIGPER
Nature of construction	NATCON	Signal sequence	SIGSEQ
Nature of surface	NATSUR	Sounding accuracy	SOUACC
Nature of surface - qualifying terms	NATQUA	Sounding distance - maximum	SDISMX
Notice to Mariners date	NMDATE	Sounding distance - minimum	SDISMN
Object name	OBJNAM		
Orientation	ORIENT	Source date	SORDAT
Periodic date end	PEREND	Source indication	SORIND
Periodic date start	PERSTA	Status	STATUS

ATTRIBUTE	ACRONYM	ATTRIBUTE	ACRONYM
Survey date - end	SUREND	Value of annual change in magnetic variation	VALACM
Survey date - start	SURSTA		
Survey type	SURTYP	Value of depth contour	VALDCO
Symbol scaling factor	$SCALE	Value of local magnetic anomaly	VALLMA
Symbolization code	$SCODE		
Technique of sounding measurement	TECSOU	Value of magnetic variation	VALMAG
		Value of maximum range	VALMXR
Text string	$TXSTR	Value of nominal range	VALNMR
Textual description	TXTDSC	Value of sounding	VALSOU
Tidal stream - panel values	TS_TSP	Vertical accuracy	VERACC
Tidal stream - time series values	TS_TSV	Vertical clearance	VERCLR
		Vertical clearance, closed	VERCCL
Tide - accuracy of water level	T_ACWL	Vertical clearance, open	VERCOP
		Vertical clearance, safe	VERCSA
Tide - high and low water values	T_HWLW	Vertical datum	VERDAT
		Vertical length	VERLEN
Tide - method of tidal prediction	T_MTOD	Water level effect	WATLEV
Tide - time and height differences	T_THDF	Information in national language	NINFOM
Tide - time series values	T_TSVL	Object name in national language	NOBJNM
Tide - value of harmonic constituents	T_VAHC	Pilot district in national language	NPLDST
Tide - time interval of values	T_TINT	Text string in national language	$NTXST
Time end	TIMEND	Textual description in national language	NTXTDS
Time start	TIMSTA		
Tint	$TINTS	Horizontal datum	HORDAT
Topmark/daymark shape	TOPSHP	Positional Accuracy	POSACC
Traffic flow	TRAFIC	Quality of position	QUAPOS

Other books by the author on ENC

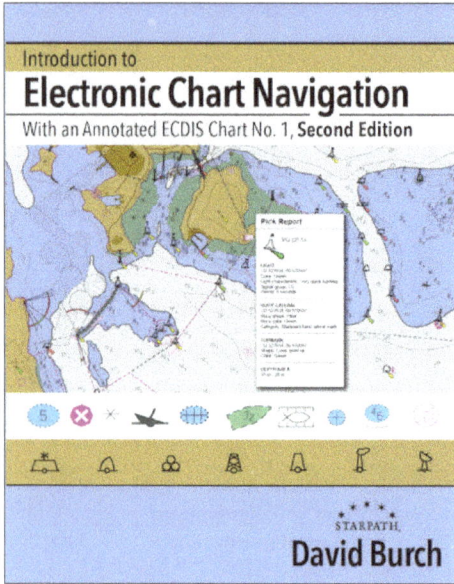

Expands on the content of the *Essentials* booklet, compares ENC with other echart formats, and adds extended discussion of safe, efficient navigation with ENC, including waypoint selection and route design, use of heading and COG predictor lines, tides and currents, and more. Full color, 154 pages, 8.5"x11". Details and support at www.starpath.com/ENC

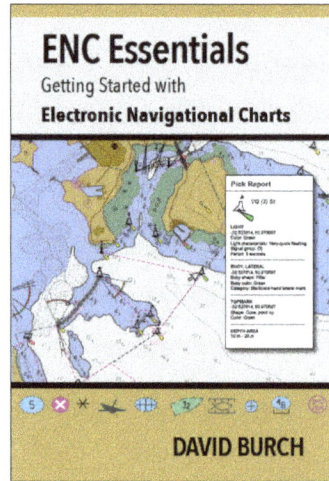

Covers the basics of ENC structure and how to read them. Full color, 50 pages, 6"x9". Details and support at www.starpath.com/ENC